Lessons from Toddlers

By Mitta Xinindlu

MITTA
XININDLU

writing to heal millions of
people

Preface

This is a special project that is meant to make us remember the lessons that we're always learning from our little gifts, our toddlers. I created this book as a working notebook. For each point, you will be able to write your ideas, memories, or wishes relating to your little angel. I know that you will have a smile on your face while working on this. Surely, you will enjoy reminiscing about your beautiful children, and all their special moments.

Parenthood is a lesson on its own. But the best lessons in parenthood are from our children. Let's cherish them, appreciate them, and recognise their special roles in our lives. Let's love our children purely. Let's protect their innocence and develop them into being individuals who are self-assured.

Our children are the extension of ourselves. If you didn't have the best upbringing, you now have a chance to make the life of your child better. And in that, you will also be healing your younger self.

Quick Guide

Chapter 1: Don't sweat the small stuff.
Chapter 2. Apologise when in the wrong.
Chapter 3: Move on. Don't dwell on it.
Chapter 4: Take naps when tired.
Chapter 5: Ask as many questions as it is necessary.

Chapter 6: Set some time off for play.
Chapter 7: Eat regularly.
Chapter 8: Be brave to express your raw emotions.
Chapter 9: Know how to get what you want.
Chapter 10: Learn the room.

Chapter 11: Listen to your instincts.
Chapter 12: Seek comfort when in need.
Chapter 13: Connect with your creative side.
Chapter 14: Be open to learning new things.
Chapter 15: Take your time to master a new skill.

Chapter 16: Be fearless.
Chapter 17: Be curious.
Chapter 18: Explore; but know your limits.
Chapter 19: Have friends.
Chapter 20: Laugh often.

Chapter 1
Don't sweat the small stuff.

1

If you make a mistake, pause. Continue with the activity at a later stage.

_____

_____

_____

_____

_____

2

It's not a big deal if you wear your shoes on the wrong foot. Laugh at yourself and fix it when you're ready.

_____

_____

_____

_____

_____

3

Drawing on the wall, or making some mess, is not a big deal. What matters is the intention behind the action. In many cases, the intention is pure.

_____

_____

_____

_____

_____

4

Touching dirt, or playing on the ground, isn't a death sentence. It's experimental and fun. Touch a bit of soil sometimes. Have a garden.

_____

_____

_____

_____

_____

5

Eating too much on a certain occasion will not contribute to your weight gain. Enjoy the deliciousness of the food without worrying about your kilos.

_____

_____

_____

_____

_____

6

A little blunder, even if many, will not tarnish your image. Mistakes are part of life.

_____

_____

_____

_____

7

If someone refuses to give you something, holding a grudge is useless.

_____

_____

_____

_____

8

Falling is part of life. But you must get up regardless of whether there is someone there to pick you up or not.

_____

_____

_____

_____

_____

9

Scratches and light wounds should not stop you from enjoying life. When people or things hurt you, have some strength to continue living your life.

_____

_____

_____

_____

_____

10

Expensive toys are nice to have. But the most fun can be the simple and cheap ones. Make the best of experiences out of the minimum resources that you may have.

Chapter 2
Apologise when in the wrong.

1

It's easy to move on from an issue when there's an apology. Apologise to others when in the wrong. If they don't apologise to you, don't let it hold you from living your best life.

_____

_____

_____

_____

2

The action of acknowledging that you were in the wrong can make others trust you.

_____

_____

_____

_____

_____

3

Follow up on the apology by offering sweet words or comforting actions.

_____

_____

_____

_____

_____

4

Once the apology has been accepted, do not repeat the same action. But if you do, due to long-term conditioning, do some self-reflection.

_____

_____

_____

_____

_____

5

Give plenty of hugs. Make sure that your hugs are appropriate and welcome. Hug some more!

_____

_____

_____

_____

_____

6

Let the people whom you appreciate know that they're important to you. Or that you value their presence.

_____

_____

_____

_____

_____

7

People are not on this earth for a long time. Don't hold grudges once you've accepted the apology.

8

A small mistake doesn't break trust or the relationship. It is the intention behind the action that does.

_____

_____

_____

_____

9

Don't assume that others know that you're upset. Explain why their actions made you upset. That will make the other person understand.

_____

_____

_____

_____

_____

10
Forgive honestly.

Chapter 3
Move on. Don't dwell on it.

1

Small behavioural irritations are part of life. No one is perfect.

_____

_____

_____

_____

_____

2

Take a few steps, fall, get up, and do it again …until you're up and running.

3

A new day opens a wide door for new opportunities to come into your life.

4

You're still angry over that action? They're already over it and have moved on. So, who's really suffering in this equation?

5

Dwelling on things causes unnecessary stress. It can make you sick too. Take care of yourself.

6

Not every rejection needs a follow-up. Sometimes seeking closure from the people who've rejected you can hurt you even more.

_____

_____

_____

_____

_____

7

It might look risky and dangerous at first, but it could be part of a big and valuable lesson.

8

Don't take everything to heart. Seriously, don't take everything to heart.

9

Be still during some of the storms or tantrums of life. They will pass. And you will fix the damage when the atmosphere is calm.

_____

_____

_____

_____

_____

10

In the end, you will look back and smile at everything.

Chapter 4
Take naps when tired.

1

The body was designed to work, and rest. Allow it to rejuvenate itself through naps and/or sleep.

2

The mind needs its break too. Meditate to rejuvenate your thinking capacity.

_____

_____

_____

_____

_____

3

Meditation is a hidden getaway
to the calmness and stillness
that our souls yearn.

_____

_____

_____

_____

4

Do not stick to a certain time. Listen to your body. Each day may be different. Your body will wake up when it's completed its retreat.

_____

_____

_____

_____

_____

5

Routines are recommended and necessary for some. But if you skip a nap at your usual time, it's okay. Don't stress.

6
Meditation is an adult's way to a toddler's daydreaming.

_____

_____

_____

_____

_____

7

Have a vision board. That's how toddlers transform pretend games into big and real success stories.

8

Speak up when you feel tired. Guard your mental health. Tell someone that you'd like a pause in your daily schedule.

9

We all need reassurance to be
able to find some good rest.
Choose your comfort method.
But don't limit yourself to one.

_____

_____

_____

_____

_____

10

Find a calm and quiet place to relax. Detaching from the noise and the business of the day is necessary.

Chapter 5
Ask as many questions as it is necessary.

1

The original inventor of the most famous five WHYs theory was a toddler. Think about it, per day, how many times does your toddler ask you the question WHY? Parents who are with their toddlers much of the day will know the answer.

2

We ask questions because we are either curious or clueless. At times, we want to give the other person some time to reflect on their statement.

3

The person who doesn't ask questions is the least intelligent one in the room.

_____

_____

_____

_____

_____

4

The more you ask questions, the bigger you grow your knowledge vault. Perhaps, also the wiser you become.

_____

_____

_____

_____

5
We got to know because we were not afraid to ask questions.

_____

_____

_____

_____

_____

6

If they don't want to answer to your questions, ask them why.

7

Ask, ask, ask away! Toddlers know no limit. That's how they grow their minds.

_____

_____

_____

_____

_____

8

If they refuse you an answer, seek another alternative from which to find your answer.

_____

_____

_____

_____

_____

9
Asking questions also indicates bravery.

_____

_____

_____

_____

_____

10

Many people suffered because they were afraid to pose the tough questions. And some were full of regret because they were afraid to ask any questions.

Chapter 6
Set some time off for play.

1

Choose any sport or entertainment that stimulates your mind and body. At least, commit to one.

_____

_____

_____

_____

_____

2
Don't play to compete. Play to have fun.

3

If it's giving you stress, it's not the right game for you.

_____

_____

_____

_____

_____

4

Play often. Play regularly. But never play all the time.

_____

_____

_____

_____

_____

5

Some games require a certain skill. Never shy away from acquiring it if you find the game worthwhile.

_____

_____

_____

_____

_____

6

Some plays are best shared with others, while some are best enjoyed alone.

_____

_____

_____

_____

_____

7

Your family members will not always be around to play with you. Also have external trusted parties.

_____

_____

_____

_____

_____

8

Have a variety of games in which you engage. Variety sharpens your cognitive skills.

_____

_____

_____

_____

_____

9

Don't be shy to play alone when others refuse to play with you, or aren't available due to other commitments.

_____

_____

_____

_____

10

Public places are for everyone to enjoy. Never allow a bully to infringe upon your right to use.

Chapter 7
Eat regularly.

1

Eating is important for your survival. But eating as a passion is a matter of a choice.

_____

_____

_____

_____

_____

2

Eat healthy foods. A healthy diet eliminates the expenses of doctor visits (and the gym).

_____

_____

_____

_____

_____

3

Eat different types of foods. Variety is the best in everything.

4

Do not shy away from eating alone. Even going to a restaurant alone is ideal.

_____

_____

_____

_____

_____

5

Do not shy away from snacking in-between the meals. If it's healthy snacks, the body will thank you.

6

Drink lots of healthy liquids. Water remains the best option.

_____

_____

_____

_____

7

Eat according to your personal rhythm. Don't hurry yourself up or slower yourself down to match others.

8

Try foods from other cultures too. Food can get you closer to knowing other people better.

_____

_____

_____

_____

_____

9

Eat with your hands. Eat with cutlery. Eat with chopsticks. As you wish.

_____

_____

_____

_____

_____

10

Mix different foods. Make your own recipes. All recipes are a discovery of a curious mind.

_____

_____

_____

_____

_____

Chapter 8
Be brave to express your raw emotions.

1

Crying, laughing, or screaming are expressions that result from felt emotions. Express yourself in the manner that is the most comfortable to you.

_____

_____

_____

_____

_____

2

Tell people when you're not feeling well. They'll either help you or give you the much-needed space. You'll win either way.

_____

_____

_____

_____

_____

3

Admitting, firstly to yourself, that you're not okay is the beginning of healing your most troubled emotions.

_____

_____

_____

_____

_____

4

The more you admit to the rawness of your emotions, the easier your heart will feel. And the clearer your life will be.

5

Every emotion wants to be expressed. Find a safe way to express the hard ones.

_____

_____

_____

_____

_____

6

Rawness is related to vulnerability. But they're not the same.

7

Look for safe people to whom you can show your vulnerability and rawness. Not everyone deserves that privilege.

_____

_____

_____

_____

_____

8

It is possible that some may use your vulnerability and rawness against you. Don't worry much. Instead put Plan B in place to combat their actions.

9

Remember how raw you were with your mother when you were a toddler? Now, remember the reaction that you received. Was it good, was it bad? Have you made any actions to resolve those feelings? Reflect on it.

10

There will come a time when being *raw* is the new norm. Don't be embarrassed for being sensitive and vulnerable. Be glad that you're alive.

_____

_____

_____

_____

_____

Chapter 9
Know how to get what you want.

1
Be kind to other people... particularly, to those on whom your survival depends.

_____

_____

_____

_____

_____

2

Smile. Your smile can soften even the hardest hearts.

3

Say 'please and thank you'. It really works in getting what you want.

_____

_____

_____

_____

_____

4

In harsh times, and as the last resort, cry yourself out. Express your desperation.

_____

_____

_____

_____

_____

5

Use different requesting methods, even if asking for the same thing.

_____

_____

_____

_____

_____

6

Tell them how important they are to you. Tell them often. [My toddler calls me her best friend when she wants something. I could never resist.]

_____

_____

_____

_____

_____

7

Use your sense of touch only with appropriate people.

8
Reject when they offer what you don't want... and use that time as an opportunity to ask for what you really want.

_____

_____

_____

_____

_____

9

Use reminders. People usually forget their promises towards you.

_____

_____

_____

_____

_____

10

Explain why you're refusing to participate in an activity. Or why you're not accepting their offer.

_____

_____

_____

_____

_____

Chapter 10
Learn the room.

1

Energies speak louder than voices. They can protect you most times, but also deceive you other times.

2

When the energy in the room doesn't feel right, probably, it's not right. But sometimes it's also because of you.

_____

_____

_____

_____

_____

3

Toddlers will attach themselves to energies that feel comfortable to them. Because energies don't lie.

_____

_____

_____

_____

_____

4

People lie and deceive but energies don't.

5

Look people in their left eye.
You'll get to know where you
stand with them much easier.

_____

_____

_____

_____

_____

6

Stand in the room. But stand with those who follow the truth. And stand against those who easily connect with the lies.

_____

_____

_____

_____

_____

7

The room could either be empty or filled with people. Either way, it's always full of energy.

_____

_____

_____

_____

8
Know when to stay or when to leave the room.

9

Some people might make you feel that you don't belong in certain spaces. The reality is that it's possible that they're the ones who don't belong there. So, don't hurry to leave when there's discomfort.

10

The rooms to explore are not limited only to the ones on planet earth. Don't be afraid to also explore the spaces above, below, within, and beyond.

_____

_____

_____

Chapter 11
Listen to your instincts.

1

Children are attuned to their basic instincts. These were made to protect them in their infancy. Listen to your instincts.

_____

_____

_____

_____

2

If an encounter with a person doesn't feel right, probably it's not right.

3

At times, we know when people are cheating us, but sadly we've become desensitised to our instincts.

_____

_____

_____

_____

_____

4

Vulnerability is the biggest attraction to all predators. But your survival instincts are also at the highest when in danger. Use them, don't let fear shut them down.

5

Fight or flight. Know when either of them is useful. Don't fight lost battles. Flee at once.

6

Your instincts will also help you recognise any red flags. Don't let your logic win in such situations.

7

There are factors that can distort your basic instincts. Such as your health status, people around you, or your mood swings. Be mindful of your situation before taking decisions based off on your instincts.

8

Not everyone is attuned to their instincts. Some choose to ignore them, while some ignore them because of trauma.

_____

_____

_____

_____

_____

9

The topic of instincts is tough to dissect. But one can gain a better understanding by observing the behaviour of animals.

_____

_____

_____

_____

_____

10

Your instincts are your gift of survival from your Creator.

Chapter 12
Seek comfort when in need.

1

The first person from whom we find our comfort is our mother. But she is not the limit.

2
Comfort foods, or any other habits, are good for you until they're bad.

3

The meaning of the word comfort is defined by you. What's comfortable to you may not be comfortable to the next person. Be mindful of that.

_____

_____

_____

_____

4

The arms of a trusted and safe person are the best gift for the full development of any person.

_____

_____

_____

_____

_____

5

Not everyone who offers you some comfort is to be trusted.

6

Some people exchange comfort for vulnerability. It's a dangerous transaction.

_____

_____

_____

_____

_____

7

Choose a trusted place or person from where you find your comfort. There is a direct relationship between trustful comfort and peace of mind.

_____

_____

_____

_____

_____

8

We all want to be comfortable in our lives. Our families should be the first source of that comfort.

_____

_____

_____

_____

9

The purest gift is someone who wants to give you comfort for nothing in return.

_____

_____

_____

_____

_____

10
Comfort is not love. But love can be comfort.

Chapter 13
Connect with your creative side.

1

Take a hobby. Explore your creative nature.

_____

_____

_____

_____

_____

2

One of the best feelings on earth is having your hands build something.

3

Art shouldn't be necessarily done for an audience. Sometimes creating for yourself can be equally rewarding.

4
Creativity helps us fulfil our purposes in this life.

_____

_____

_____

_____

_____

5

Draw, dance, invent, plan, or do something amusing to stimulate your imagination.

_____

_____

_____

_____

_____

6

Seek people with whom you can either create or share your creation.

_____

_____

_____

_____

_____

7

Being creative, in any form, gives magical power to an individual. One transforms from being just a person to being a creator.

_____

_____

_____

_____

_____

8
There is a parallel relationship between being creative and being intelligent.

_____

_____

_____

_____

_____

9

Creativity enhances all your senses. And the best part is that one also gets to dabble into their sixth sense as well.

10
Creativity doesn't require competition. Do it for you or for a good cause.

_____

_____

_____

_____

_____

Chapter 14
Be open to learning new things.

1

The first step to learning new things is the realisation that we don't know. Some get stuck on this step, and some never arrive to it. Some get to advance to the second step, which is accepting that we don't know. Thereafter, some will further advance into seeking knowledge to fill the gap. Then, some will seek understanding of that knowledge. From that group, which is usually only a few individuals, some will apply that understanding to obtain results. But the process doesn't end there. Because some will analyse those results. Then after that, some will report the results for others to gain insight. Then the cycle starts again. In the end, the question is: where are you in this process of learning?

2
Learning something doesn't guarantee that you'll retain the knowledge forever.

3

As studies have shown, there's a difference between data, information, and knowledge. Always assess what you're gaining.

4

Be open to learning new things. That's how we grow and evolve.

5
Discernment and learning are best friends. One should never desert the other.

6

Any improvement comes through openness and willingness.

_____

_____

_____

_____

_____

7

Not all lessons are meant to help you. Some are presented to you to distract you from reaching your destiny. A shoemaker's technical lessons are not so
useful to a fruit seller.

8

Spend as much time on lessons as needed. You don't want to have any regrets.

9

Be open to share and receive lessons. It's a cycle of life.

_____

_____

_____

_____

_____

10

Utilise the internet to gain more knowledge. Most times people are busy completing their own lessons to teach you everything that you need to know.

_____

_____

_____

_____

Chapter 15
Take your time to master a new skill.

1

Nothing is known in a minute.
Nothing is known in one shot.

2

Things could be messy and clumsy the first time you try something. But with time, the mess starts to disappear.

3

Just like a sculptor takes time to mould a sculpture, take your time to hone your skills too.

_____

_____

_____

_____

4

There is no set time for a skill to be attained. Each skill is required uniquely to each person, and at a certain time.

_____

_____

_____

_____

5

Other people could be comparing your progress to those of others. But you're walking your unique path. You should be concerned mostly about your development. The external pressure is unnecessary.

6

Try different activities to see which skill is best suitable for your success path. Without variety, you'll never know.

7

They say that Rome wasn't built in one day. And nothing is built in one day. Even if an action happens in one day, the planning took place in the mind days, months, or even years before.

8
it's your own pace, race, and phase.

9
Learn, build, and master.

_____

_____

_____

_____

_____

10
Indeed, even if one masters the skill, there's always a room for advancement.

Chapter 16
Be fearless.

1

Be fearless …just like a toddler who jumps out of his bed, seeking freedom or reassurance.

_____

_____

_____

_____

_____

2
Fear can be good. But when bad, it is detrimental.

3
We advance in life when we let the fear go.

_____

_____

_____

_____

4

We grow into new versions of ourselves when we eliminate the fear within. Some never travel because of fear. Some die with untold stories because of fear. Some remain imprisoned in their minds because of fear. Let the fear go.

_____

_____

_____

5

The child is born free of fear. But it is the feelings or actions of the parents, or those around, that instil the spirit of fear in the child.

_____

_____

_____

_____

_____

6

Without fear, we can be unstoppable in our endeavours.

7

Imagine how great of the heights you would mount if fear was not an issue.

_____

_____

_____

_____

_____

8
Some infringe upon their own human rights due to fear. It's sad.

9
Fear is the number one enemy to any progress.

_____

_____

_____

_____

_____

10
When you let go of the fear, liberation takes place.

_____

_____

_____

_____

_____

Chapter 17
Be curious.

1
Curiosity is the root of invention.

---

*

2
Be curious but be mindful.

3

The development of our senses grows because of curiosity. We smell something, then, we progress to tasting or touching it. Or vice versa.

4

Feed a child's curious mind with knowledge and wisdom. Then, the result will truly be based on their choice.

5

Sometimes we talk to people because we're curious about whom they are. Imagine how limited our individual worlds would be without being curious.

6
Being curious is an indication of being alive.

_____

_____

_____

_____

_____

7

We could never know what works best for us if we weren't curious.

_____

_____

_____

_____

_____

8

Travellers travel because of curiosity. Explorers explore because of curiosity. Anything good that we have is due to curiosity. But, so as the bad.

_____

_____

_____

_____

_____

9

There are beautiful doors to which that your curiosity can lead you. Use your instincts when choosing which one to open.

_____

_____

_____

_____

_____

10

Take every day lightly. Not all your curiosity needs to be fulfilled at once.

_____

_____

_____

_____

_____

Chapter 18
Explore, but know your limits.

1

Touch the fire and you will burn your hands. But if you observe the density of the heat before you touch it, you will save your hands.

2

Many times, we're told not to explore what we want. And sometimes it is for a good reason. At times, it is either for our protection or for the protection of others.

3

The law is, at most times, the best measure of our limitations.

4

The mind knows know limitations, but your body does.

5

Listen to good advice and kind warnings. They're for your benefit.

_____

_____

_____

_____

6

In your exploration, observe, analyse, reflect, and beware.

_____

_____

_____

_____

7

Not every field is worth digging.
Preserve your energy and time
for worthwhile missions.

8
When exploring, read the warning signs: figuratively and literally.

9

Sometimes the dangerous places are not marked. Be sure to use your senses in such situations.

_____

_____

_____

_____

_____

10
Remain in your lane. But only in times of danger.

_____

_____

_____

_____

Chapter 19
Have friends.

1

Classify your friends into groups. Classify them per their roles in your life. It will save you from investing on the wrong people.

2

Friends can be the best place for support. They can also be insightful and delightful to you.

_____

_____

_____

_____

3
Friends can be the family you never had.

4

Not all friends are worthy of your immediate attention. Remember that bad friends are still in the category of 'friends'.

_____

_____

_____

_____

_____

5

Some friends may want to show their dominance over you. Thread lightly.

6
Friendship is not supposed to hurt.

7

If they don't consider your needs, they aren't real friends.

_____

_____

_____

_____

_____

8

Friendship should be fair. It becomes charity if you're always the giver and the other person the receiver ...and without reciprocation.

_____

_____

_____

_____

9

We make time for our friends. But plan the time right so that you don't neglect your own needs.

_____

_____

_____

_____

_____

10

You don't need many friends to feel appreciated. One good one is enough. In most times, lean on yourself. You're your best friend first.

_____

_____

_____

_____

Chapter 20
Laugh often.

1

Not everything has to be taken seriously. But not everything is funny either.

_____

_____

_____

_____

_____

2

Laugh at small things, small mistakes, or small gestures.

3

Share your jokes with people who will understand, not with people whom you're trying to impress.

_____

_____

_____

_____

4

Laughter is not an indication of happiness.

5

When people say they laugh often together, it could indicate an easy feeling between the connection of their energies. Or it could also indicate that there are no serious issues to discuss.

6

Not everyone who laughs with you is on your side. Some do it to make you a prey to their evil plans.

7
Laugh often. But also laugh genuinely.

_____

_____

_____

_____

_____

8

Recognise the type of laughter that you receive. Some people laugh when they're intensely irritated. Not necessarily because they find you amusing.

_____

_____

_____

_____

9

There is a beautiful paradox between laughter and tears. I wish that you'll laugh until your tears flood your face. All because you're truly happy.

_____

_____

_____

_____

_____

10
Remember that in the end, those who laughed the hardest did not prove to be the happiest.

Outro

Dear my sweet daughter,

Thank you for the good memories, and the wise lessons that I learnt through having you in my life. I knew somethings before your arrival. But I know better things today. I love you fiercely. I love you forever.

Keep in touch!

www.mittaxinindlu.com

www.facebook.com/MittaXinindluAuthor

www.ingramcontent.com/pod-product-compliance
Lightning Source LLC
Chambersburg PA
CBHW031127090426
42738CB00008B/1003